Thanks so Dr Murray Simons and craig Brown for your assistance putting this book together.
ISBN: 979-85685-610-7-1

To my friends and family at Beyond Grappling Club

Gewidmet meiner Familie sowie Freunden des Beyond Grappling Clubs

History of Judo For Kids

Die Geschichte von Judo für Kinder

Written by Matt D'Aquino
Illustrated by Craig Brown

A long time ago in Japan, strong samurai warriors walked the streets. They were heroes in their towns and villages, and used jiu jitsu fighting techniques to challenge each other to see who the strongest fighter was.

In Japan gingen vor langer Zeit starke Samurai-Krieger durch die Straßen. Sie waren Helden in ihren Städten und Dörfern und verwendeten Jujutsu-Kampftechniken, um sich gegenseitig zu fordern und herauszufinden, wer der stärkere Kämpfer war.

During this time, a young man named Jigoro Kano was getting bullied at school. This was because he was smaller than everyone else. Someone told Kano that he should learn jiu jitsu techniques so he could defend himself.

Zu dieser Zeit wurde ein junger Mann mit dem Namen Jigoro Kano in der Schule schikaniert. Der Grund dafür war, dass er kleiner war als alle anderen. Man sagte Kano, er solle Jujutsu-Techniken lernen, damit er sich wehren könne.

Kano found a Sensei and began an intense training regime. Everyday he went to the training to learn how to fall safely, throw, trip, and sweep someone to the ground.

Kano traf einen Sensei (oder Lehrer) und startete ein hartes Trainingsprogramm. Tagtäglich ging er ins Dojo, um dort zu lernen, wie man sicher fällt, wirft, stolpert und andere zu Boden wirft.

He also worked hard to learn holds, escapes and joint locks while fighting on the ground.

Außerdem arbeitete er hart daran, Griffe, Fluchten und Gelenksperren zu erlernen, während er am Boden kämpfte.

He became highly skilled in only a few years, due to his dedication to learning and consistent training. After putting many techniques into practice, he discovered that a lot of them only worked if you were bigger and stronger than your opponent. This meant that someone of Kano's small size was at a disadvantage.

In nur wenigen Jahren wurde Kano dank seiner Hingabe zum Lernen und seiner ständigen Weiterbildung hoch qualifiziert. Nachdem er viele Techniken in die Tat umgesetzt hatte, stellte er fest, dass viele von ihnen nur dann funktionierten, wenn man größer und stärker als sein Gegenüber war. Dies hatte zur Folge, dass jemand von Kanos kleiner Größe im Nachteil war.

He made it his mission to improve the techniques he was taught. Using his knowledge of how the human body moves and his love for studying other grappling arts, he began dissecting each technique in detail. He altered them in a way that allowed technique to overcome strength when applied with correct leverage and timing.

Kano hat es sich zur Aufgabe gemacht, die ihm gelehrten Techniken zu verbessern. Mit seinem Wissen darüber, wie sich der menschliche Körper fortbewegt, und seiner Liebe zum Studium anderer Greiftechniken begann er, jede Technik im Detail zu untersuchen. Er änderte sie in einer Art und Weise, die es der Technik ermöglichte, die Kraft zu überwinden, sofern sie mit der richtigen Hebelwirkung und dem richtigen Timing ausgeführt wurde.

After years of study Kano put his new and improved techniques into an easy to follow system. In 1882, he opened his very own Judo school which he called the Kodokan. Kano's new grappling art was known as Kano Jiu Jitsu or Kodokan Judo.

Nach jahrelangem Lernen hat Kano seine neuen und verbesserten Techniken in ein leicht nachvollziehbares System gebracht. Im Jahre 1882 gründete er seine eigene Judoschule, die er Kodokan nannte. Kanos neue Greifkunst war unter dem Namen Kano Jujutsu oder Kodokan Judo bekannt.

Kano's system combined what he thought was the best parts of the jiu jitsu he studied. The three founding principles are:

- Maximum efficiency, minimum effort: using minimal energy or strength to defeat a bigger, stronger person.
- Mutual welfare, mutual benefit: living and training in a way that benefits everyone.
- Strive for perfection: Trying to be a better person embracing honesty, kindness and teamwork in everyday life.

Kanos System verband das, was er für die besten Teile des Jujutsu hielt, das er studierte. Die drei Grundprinzipien sind:

- *Gegenseitiges Wohlbefinden zum gegenseitigen Vorteil (Leben und Ausbildung in einer Weise, die jedem zugute kommt)*
- *Maximale Effizienz, minimale Anstrengung (minimale Energie oder Kraft aufwenden, um eine größere, kräftigere Person zu besiegen)*
- *Strebe für Perfektion!!. Versuche eine bessere Person zu sein die Ehrlichkeit, Freundlichkeit und das Teamwork im täglichen Leben schätzt.*

Kano began teaching his martial art to everyone who wanted to learn— boys, girls, big people, little people, even old people. He developed it in such a way that you could practice really hard without getting hurt. To do this he removed or changed dangerous techniques and taught everyone how to fall safely. But most of all, he taught everyone to show respect to each other. He also emphasized the fact that Judo is more than just sport; it is a way of life.

Kano fing an, seine Kampfkunst allen zu lehren, die es lernen wollten - Jungen, Mädchen, große Menschen, kleine Menschen, sogar alte Menschen. Er hat die Kampfkunst derart entwickelt, dass man wirklich hart trainieren konnte, ohne verletzt zu werden. Dazu entfernte oder änderte er bestimmte gefährliche Kampftechniken und brachte allen bei, wie man fällt, ohne sich zu verletzen. Vor allem aber brachte er allen bei, sich gegenseitig Respekt zu zeigen. Er unterstrich auch die Tatsache, dass Judo mehr als nur Sport ist; es ist eine Lebenseinstellung.

Over time Judo became very popular in Japan, and it was taken to other countries by Kano's students. Today, it is practiced in nearly every country in the world.

Im Laufe der Zeit wurde Judo in Japan sehr beliebt, und es wurde von Kanos Schülern in weitere Länder getragen. Heutzutage wird es in fast jedem Land der Welt ausgeübt.

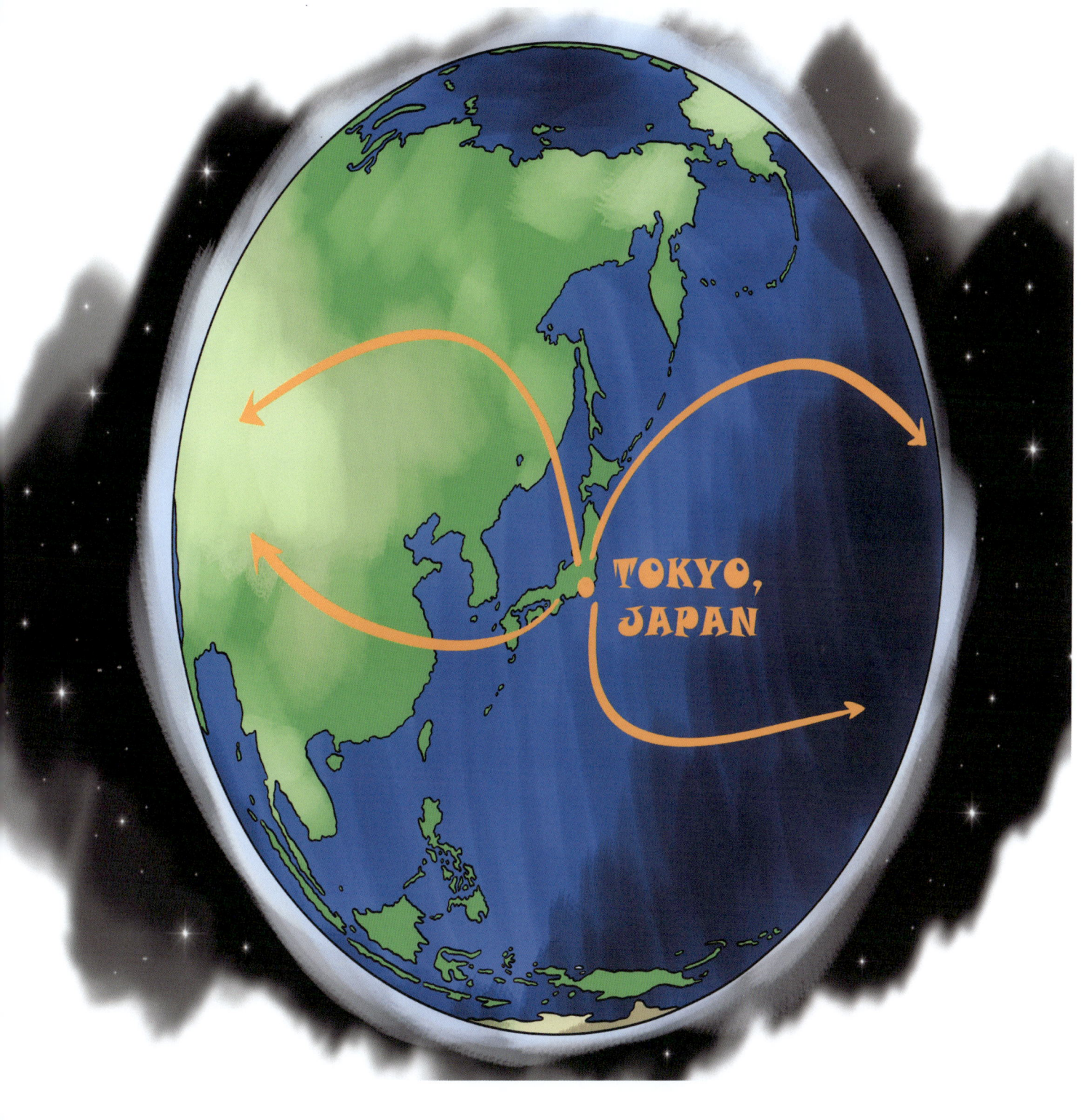

Judo training is a great place to have fun, make friends, develop self-confidence, self-discipline and learn effective self-defence techniques. There many ways you can be involved in Judo. You can do team and individual competition, kata, refereeing, coaching or simply train each week and have fun.

Das Judotraining bietet viel Spaß, schafft Freundschaften und fördert Selbstvertrauen, Selbstdisziplin und das Erlernen wirksamer Selbstverteidigungstechniken. Es gibt zahlreiche Möglichkeiten, sich am Judo zu beteiligen. Sie können Team- und Einzelwettbewerbe, Kata, Schiedsrichter, Coaching oder einfach jede Kommen sie Woche trainieren und dabei auch noch Spaß haben.

We are so thankful for Kano's incredible ability to learn, study and develop such a great martial art. His perseverance and strength of character is something that many Judoka strive for.

Wir sind unglaublich dankbar für Kanos enorme Fähigkeit, eine so großartige Kampfkunst zu erlernen, zu erforschen und zu entwickeln. Seine Durchhaltevermögen und Charakterstärke ist etwas, das viele Judoka erreichen wollen.

About the Author:

Matt D'Aquino is a Judo Olympian and author from Canberra, Australia. He has represented Australia at eight Continental Championships, four World Championships and competed in the 2008 Beijing Olympic Games. He is also a Brazilian Jiu jitsu Black Belt.

Matt is passionate about teaching and has helped thousands of grapplers worldwide through his online Judo resources, eBooks and online content which can be found at beyondgrappling.com and universityofjudo.com

About the Illustrator:

Craig Brown is a digital media professional and freelance artist based in the Northern Territory, Australia. Craig is a judoka with over ten years of experience in Judo, currently training and coaching at Top End Judo Academy. He loves Judo almost as much as he loves drawing, as Judo completely changed his life for the better.

Printed in Poland
by Amazon Fulfillment
Poland Sp. z o.o., Wrocław

23727788R00018